SCIENCE Q&A

SPORTS

— Jayne Creighton —

Weigl Publishers Inc.

Published by Weigl Publishers Inc.
350 5th Avenue, Suite 3304, PMB 6G
New York, NY 10118-0069

Website: www.weigl.com

All of the Internet URLs given in the book were valid at the time of publication. However, due to the dynamic nature of the Internet, some addresses may have changed, or sites may have ceased to exist since publication. While the author and publisher regret any inconvenience this may cause readers, no responsibility for any such changes can be accepted by either the author or the publisher.

Library of Congress Cataloging-in-Publication Data available upon request.
Fax 1-866-44-WEIGL for the attention of the Publishing Records department.

ISBN 978-1-60596-070-8 (hard cover)
ISBN 978-1-60596-071-5 (soft cover)

Printed in China
1 2 3 4 5 6 7 8 9 0 13 12 11 10 09

Project Coordinator
Heather C. Hudak

Design
Terry Paulhus

Photo credits
Weigl acknowledges Getty Images as its primary image supplier for this title.

Every reasonable effort has been made to trace ownership and to obtain permission to reprint copyright material. The publishers would be pleased to have any errors or omissions brought to their attention so that they may be corrected in subsequent printings.

CONTENTS

4   What is a sport?

6   How do muscles affect running?

8   Why do we breathe harder and sweat during exercise?

10   Why is it important to warm up before exercising?

12   How does science help swimmers?

14   What makes a boomerang come back?

16   Why do balls bounce?

18   How does better equipment help results?

20   How important is clothing to performance and safety?

22   Are sports drinks better than water?

24   What are steroids?

26   Why does my bike stay up when I am pedaling?

28   How do surfers stay on their boards?

30   Do ice skaters become dizzy when they spin?

32   How does a pitcher outsmart a batter?

34   How can a karate chop break a board?

36   How do animals play a role in sports?

38   What are extreme sports?

40   What are human machines?

42   Are kids more prone to injury than adults?

44   Sports Careers

45   Young scientists at work

46   Take a science survey

47   Fast Facts

48   Glossary/Index

What is a sport?

A sport is a game or activity that is governed by a set of rules or customs and is often engaged in competitively. Sports commonly refer to activities where the physical capabilities of the competitor determine if he or she will excel at the game. Science is all around us when we participate in sports. When you ride a bike or play basketball, you use the laws of physics. When you flex your biceps, biology is involved. When you work out and get thirsty, chemical changes in your body tell you that you need water. So, being a good athlete takes more than talent, it also takes science.

How do muscles affect running?

Muscles are made of many tiny cells called fibers. There are two different kinds of fibers that make up the muscles that are attached to bones. These are called **slow-twitch** and **fast-twitch fibers**.

find it quick

Learn more about children and running at **www.acefitness.org/fitfacts**.

Slow-twitch fibers are dark in color and are used for endurance sports such as long distance running, cycling, or gymnastics. They have a rich blood supply and a good ability to produce energy. Fast-twitch fibers are pale and are able to contract very quickly. They are used when the body needs to move quickly, such as while playing football or sprinting. However, fast-twitch fibers tire easily.

People are born with different proportions of slow-twitch and fast-twitch muscle fibers. Scientists have taken samples of muscle tissue from different athletes. Studies have found that sprinters' leg muscles consist of about 65 percent fast-twitch fibers. While long distance runners' muscles consist of about 75 percent slow-twitch fibers. These differences partly explain why sprinters can run fast for short distances only, and marathon runners can run slowly for long distances.

Muscle fibers are not the only reason for differences in speed. Strength, natural

■ The slow-twitch muscle fibers are more effective at using oxygen. They generate more fuel for continuous muscle contractions over a long time. Therefore, slow-twitch fibers are great at helping athletes run marathons and bicycle for hours.

ability, and endurance also play a vital role. However, while strength and endurance can be improved with training, we cannot change the kinds of muscle fiber in our bodies.

Grin and Bear It

Endurance exercises like running or cycling make your muscles stronger and less likely to get tired.

Why do we breathe harder and sweat during exercise?

Muscles need oxygen to take energy from food. This energy helps us to move faster. During exercise, muscles use more oxygen than when they are at rest. The body keeps its temperature down by releasing moisture from sweat glands.

Oxygen comes from the air we breathe and travels throughout the body in our blood. During exercise, muscles use more oxygen than when they are at rest. For working muscles to get enough oxygen, lungs must breathe deeper and faster. When muscles work steadily for long periods of time, they must have a constant supply of oxygen. Exercise involving such steady activity over long periods of time is called **aerobic** activity.

Muscles can get a little energy from sugar without using oxygen. This energy allows muscles to perform short, intense bursts of activity. When muscles work for very short times without using oxygen, this is called **anaerobic** activity. However, muscles pay a price for this activity. When oxygen is not available fast enough, a by-product called lactic acid builds up in the muscles. Lactic acid causes muscles to become sore.

Bodies also have a built-in thermostat at the base of the brain. This thermostat, called the **hypothalamus**, makes sure everything stays at the same temperature, about 98.6°F (37°C). When people exercise, their muscles produce heat. If the body becomes too hot, it may stop working properly. When people sweat, the moisture is warm, just like the body, and it evaporates into the air. As the sweat evaporates, it removes some of the body's excess heat. Sweating is the best way for a body to cool itself.

■ Wrestlers and other athletes have more blood flow through their lungs than non-athletes.

Why is it important to warm up before exercising?

More people are taking to exercise for a healthier life, but it is important to prepare the body before making it perform any strenuous actions.

A

A proper warmup can increase the blood flow to the muscles, which results in decreased muscle stiffness, less risk of injury, and improved performance.

Science is helping people to understand how a good diet and exercise improve their health and add enjoyment to their life. Athletes know more now about how to have the best workout without overworking their heart, lungs, and muscles, and causing injury. They understand how important it is to stretch and warm up before exercising and to stretch and cool down after a workout.

Warming up sends blood flowing into the muscles and makes them looser and less likely to tear while playing a sport. Stretching also keeps the muscles, ligaments, and tendons around joints flexible. A five-minute routine will increase flexibility and decrease soreness. Before running, for example, you can warm up your muscles by walking or jogging slowly for a few minutes.

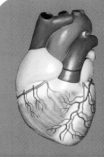

Heart Beats

The heart is a large muscle. Like other muscles, it becomes stronger with exercise. The heart of a fit person does not have to pump as often as the heart of a person who does not exercise.

How does science help swimmers?

As the sport of swimming has developed, swimmers have used their knowledge of science to reduce drag, which is the force of water. Improving swimming techniques has been the most important tool for reducing drag.

Even though water is not a solid, it creates resistance to movement. Swimmers must use force to push water out of the way. As they swim, another force, called drag, is produced. Drag is the force that occurs when a fluid, such as water, slides over a surface and seems to pull on the surface. Drag always works against the motion of the swimmer in water. Changes in swimwear have helped reduce drag. For example, wearing swim caps and smooth, tight swimsuits allows water to flow over the body more easily.

Air also exerts a force that can slow down fast-moving objects. This force is called air resistance. In some sports, air resistance hinders performance.

In a racing sport like downhill skiing, air resistance is a major obstacle. To reduce the effects of air resistance while speeding down a hill, skiers crouch into

■ Salt water is more dense and more buoyant than fresh water, so people use less energy when they swim in the sea than when they swim in a pool.

a rounded "egg" position. They also wear smooth, tight-fitting clothing that allows the air to glide over them.

Bicycle racing is another sport in which air resistance is a problem. To counter the force of air resistance, cycles have special wheels, handlebars, and helmets that are designed to let air flow smoothly over and around them.

An Olympic Feat

In 1968, the **Olympic Games** were held in Mexico City, which is more than 1 mile (1.6 km) above sea level. At such a high altitude, the air is thin and there is less air resistance. Because of this, runners ran a little more than 2 percent faster than they did at sea level. Many world records were set at these Olympic Games in the running events, like pole vault, long jump, and triple jump.

What makes a boomerang come back?

Boomerangs were invented by the Australian Aborigines many years ago. They were originally used as weapons for hunting small birds, as well as for sport.

There are two kinds of boomerangs. One is a return boomerang, and the other is a non-return boomerang. The non-return boomerang is heavier and larger, measuring 24 to 36 inches (61 to 91 cm). It was developed to hunt large game, such as kangaroos, and to be used as a weapon in war. The return boomerang is about 12 to 30 inches (30 to 76 cm) long and is shaped in a "V." One side is flat, and the other side is slightly curved, much like the wing of an airplane. The boomerang is held vertically in the right hand, with the flat part in the palm of the hand. It is thrown forward. When thrown forward, the boomerang rises, curves to the left, and glides back to the thrower. The upper wing experiences a greater lift than the lower wing. Lift is the force that pushes an airplane wing upward.

When a boomerang is spinning and moving forward at the same time, the unbalanced lift on the wings of the boomerang causes it to curve around and return to the thrower.

Some people have been able to throw a boomerang as far as 300 feet (91 m) before it returned.

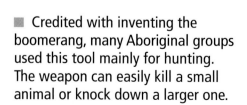

■ Credited with inventing the boomerang, many Aboriginal groups used this tool mainly for hunting. The weapon can easily kill a small animal or knock down a larger one.

Why do balls bounce?

When a ball hits the floor, it becomes slightly flattened. As the ball returns to its original shape, the energy that was stored when it hit the ground changes back into kinetic energy which is energy that is produced by motion, and it bounces upward.

An object that is being held above the ground has the potential to fall toward Earth. For this reason, it is said to have potential, or stored energy. As the object falls toward the ground, its stored energy changes into **kinetic energy**. The amount of energy that can be stored by a ball when it hits the ground depends on what the ball is made of. A rubber ball can store more energy than one made with a less "elastic" material. For example, a rubber tennis ball bounces higher than a leather baseball because it is able to store more potential energy. Most balls do not bounce back as high as they were dropped. This is because not all of the potential energy changes back into kinetic energy. Some turns into heat energy when the ball touches the floor. Some of the energy also changes into sound energy—that is what you hear when the ball hits the floor.

■ The hardwood floors used in basketball are very springy, as is an inflated basketball. When a firm basketball hits on a hardwood floor, it bounces well.

Shooting Hoops

Both Canadians and Americans can say that their country was responsible for the origin of basketball. The man who invented the game was a Canadian, Dr. James Naismith. He was a physical education teacher in Massachusetts when he was asked to invent an indoor game for his students. Dr. Naismith came up with the idea of shooting balls through peach baskets.

How does better equipment help results?

Athletes today are very fortunate. They have better pools to swim in, better fields to play on, better shoes to run in, and better bats, clubs, and rackets to hit with than ever before.

Improved equipment created from humanmade materials has greatly affected the results of many sports. This has helped athletes to continually break sports records.

In the first modern Olympic Games in 1896, the record pole vaulter reached a height of 10 feet 10 inches (3.3 m) using a wooden pole. In 1940, a man named Cornelius Warmerdan cleared 15 feet (4.5 m) using a bamboo pole. Today, using springy **fiberglass** poles, athletes are able to clear more than 19 feet (5.7 m).

There have been many other innovations in sports equipment. At the 1996 Olympic Games, rowers pulled newly designed oars with hatchet-shaped blades that move more water. Softball players can hit balls farther with bats made from ultra-light metals. Divers now use boards that provide 15 percent more spring than diving boards that were used in the 1960s.

■ The modern pole vaulting technique was developed in the United States at the end of the nineteenth century.

Improvements in time for the 100-Meter Run		
Year	Men	Women
1896	12.0 seconds	12.2 seconds
1936	10.3 seconds	11.5 seconds
1968	9.95 seconds	11.08 seconds
1992	9.96 seconds	10.82 seconds
2008	9.69 seconds	10.78 seconds

How important is clothing to performance and safety?

The invention of new humanmade materials used in clothing has had a larg
impact on sports. In addition to being comfortable to wear, these materials
may help to improve an athlete's performance. Also, today, both professiona
and amateur athletes wear special clothing and equipment to help protect
them from injury.

find it quick

Get advice on training, see photos, and read
stories about running shoes and other
equipment at **www.kidsrunning.com**.

Many athletes, such as speed skaters and bobsledders, wear spandex, a synthetic material. Spandex is a thin, synthetic, stretchable, and warm material that allows athletes to move faster than ever because it reduces air resistance.

Sometimes natural fabrics work just as well as humanmade materials in sports. Silk provides good insulation from the cold as well as protection from the Sun. Some athletes wear silk clothes under jackets that are made of a synthetic fiber that blocks the wind and rain, but allows moisture in the form of sweat to escape.

Helmets are worn in many sports. They are made with built-in shock absorbers to protect the head in case of contact with another player or a fall. Safety glasses are worn in many court sports, such as squash and racquetball, to protect the eyes. Elbow pads and

■ Rock climbers need to have clothes that help flexibility and are suitable to the weather conditions.

kneepads protect joints when people use in-line skates. Life jackets, worn during many water sports, have saved thousands of lives.

Here is your challenge!

For this challenge you need a pencil, paper, stopwatch and ruler. Measure 50 yards (46 m). Run the distance three times, wearing a different set of clothes each time. Record the time you take. Compare it, and decide which clothes help to improve your running time. For the first run, wear a T-shirt, pants, a heavy coat, and boots. For the second run, wear a sweatshirt, pants, and street shoes. In the last run, wear a T-shirt, shorts, and running shoes.

Are sports drinks better than water?

The natural choice for **hydration** is water. It is more effective than any other liquid, both before and during exercise.

When people sweat, their bodies lose water and electrolytes. If people lose too much water, they can suffer from dehydration. Dehydration can lead to fatigue and increase the chances of cramps, heat exhaustion, and heat stroke.

Electrolytes are minerals that are very important to the body. Two of these minerals are sodium (salt) and potassium. Sodium helps the body hold on to water. Sodium, calcium, and potassium are all necessary for nerves and muscles to work properly.

For some intense sports that last longer, sports drinks may be better. Sports drinks contain water for rehydration, sugar for energy, and electrolytes to replace those lost in sweat.

■ Drinking two to three glasses of water within two hours after you are done exercising replenishes the body of lost fluids.

Water Versus Sports Drinks

If you work out for fewer than 60 minutes, water is all you need. If you work out for longer than 60 minutes, sports drinks become more useful.

What are steroids?

Both professional and amateur athletes want to improve their strength and performance in sports. They want to be as strong and as fast as possible. Some people believe that taking drugs will help them become better athletes.

find it
quick

Learn more about steroids at **www.usdoj.gov/dea/ concern/steroids.html**.

■ Steroids can be dangerous and are often banned from use by professional athletes.

Some athletes take anabolic steroids in the hope of improving their performance. This drug is an artificial type of hormone. Hormones are chemicals that everyone produces naturally in their bodies, but in small amounts.

Anabolic steroids stimulate muscles into taking in more protein, and they help athletes train harder by helping them recover faster after a workout.

However, there are a number of problems connected with using steroids in sports. Drugs can cause liver damage, high blood pressure, and high cholesterol. Steroids can affect the brain and other parts of the body, and increase the risk of illness. They can also affect moods, making people more aggressive and irritable.

Side Effects

Steroid abuse has been associated with cardiovascular disease, including heart attack and stroke, even for athletes under the age of 30.

Why does my bike stay up when I am pedaling?

Do you sometimes fall or tip over when you are on your bike? This is because the wheels are not turning fast enough to keep the bike moving forward.

find it quick

Learn more about bicycles and balance at **www.wisegeek.com/why-isnt-it-harder-to-balance-on-a-bicycle.htm**.

Mountain biking involves riding bicycles off-road, often over rough terrain.

The wheels of a bicycle are two gyroscopes. A gyroscope is a spinning wheel mounted on a frame. When the wheel of a gyroscope is spinning, it resists any change in direction, and keeps the bike stable.

You probably remember when you first learned to ride a bicycle without training wheels. It took time to learn to keep your balance. Once you mastered balance, you were able to pedal faster and stay on your bike more easily.

When the wheels of a bike are spinning, it resists change in direction, and this helps the bike to stay upright. In fact, the faster the bicycle goes, the easier it is to maintain balance.

Bike Lingo

Mountain bike riders use many interesting words to describe their sport and its athletes. For example, a badly bent wheel is called a "potato chip" because of its wavy edge.

How do surfers stay on their boards?

Balance is important for many sports. In some sports, such as surfing, snowboarding, waterskiing, and skateboarding, balance is crucial.

find it quick

Learn more about surfing at **adventure. howstuffworks.com/surfing.htm**.

■ In waterskiing, an individual wears one or more skis and is pulled through the water behind a motorboat.

Just watching surfers riding the waves can be interesting. It is incredible that they are able to stand up on a small, thin board when it is moving so quickly through the waves. With practice, surfers learn to keep their balance.

Maintaining balance is connected to a person's center of gravity. Every person and object has one. The center of gravity is the point where an object can be balanced. Most men have a higher center of gravity than women have because they have wider and heavier shoulders. Surfers learn to balance when they have found their center of gravity in relation to the board.

To demonstrate center of gravity, lay a pencil across an outstretched finger. The place where it balances perfectly is the pencil's center of gravity.

Surfer King

Surfing originated in Hawaii, where it was a part of competitions for Hawaiian chiefs to demonstrate their strength and agility.

Do ice skaters become dizzy when they spin?

Everyone, including ice skaters, gets dizzy when they spin. When people spin, their eyes tell the brain one thing, and their sense of balance tells the brain another. Ice skaters learn how to get their balance back by focusing on a still object.

Balance is sensed by three tiny canals deep inside the ear. These canals are curled in loops and are filled with fluid. When the head or body starts moving or stops moving, the fluid pushes on tiny hairlike sensors in the canals. These sensors send a message to the brain, telling it what the body is doing.

When a person spins quickly and then stops, it takes time for the fluid in the ear to stop moving, just as water in a spinning cup continues to move for a few seconds after the cup has stopped. People feel dizzy because the brain is still receiving signals that say the body is spinning.

When ice skaters stop spinning, they focus very quickly on a stationary object. They also learn to concentrate very hard while their brain sorts out some mixed messages. Doing these things helps them control their dizziness.

■ While ice skating, it is important to center the body directly over the ice skate blade. This helps the skater maintain his or her balance.

Stone-Age Skates

The oldest-known pair of skates is 2,000 years old. Historians have found writing in Old Norse that describes bone runners tied to feet with thongs. These runners were probably made from the ribs of reindeer.

How does a pitcher outsmart a batter?

A good baseball pitcher knows how to put different spins on a ball to make the batter strike out. He or she knows how to throw a ball so that it curves in an unpredictable direction.

find it quick

Find the answers to sports science questions at **www.scorescience. humboldt.k12.ca.us/ fast/kids.htm**.

Aerodynamics is the science of the movement of objects through the air. A ball spinning through the air is affected by the laws of aerodynamics. These laws determine the way a ball will move through the air, how far it will go, and how fast it will travel.

As a ball spins, it is surrounded by a layer of air. The stitches on a baseball, the dimples on a golf ball, and the fuzz on a tennis ball help to grab hold of this layer of air. The way an athlete throws or hits a ball will determine its spin. That spin is also affected by different movements of air acting on the ball.

Have you ever been on a moving boat and noticed how the water churns up in a "V" shape behind the boat? This is called a wake. The same thing happens when a ball moves through the air. Only the wake behind a baseball is invisible.

Underspin (backspin)

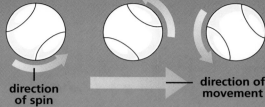

direction of spin — direction of movement

An underspin, or backspin, produces faster-moving air on top of the ball and slower-moving air under the ball. This combination pulls the ball upward.

Overspin

An overspin produces faster-moving air under the ball. This pulls the ball downward.

Sidespin

On a sidespin, air is moving faster across one side of the ball, which makes it move sideways. This is the most unpredictable pitch that can be thrown.

Here is your challenge!

For this challenge, run across a field with a large sheet of card paper held in front of you or ride a bicycle into the wind. Discuss what you experience as you run across the field or ride against the wind. Try to explain what is happening in terms of air resistance.

How can a karate chop break a board?

It is hard to imagine how a karate chop from a human hand can break a wooden board or a block of concrete. When a great deal of force is concentrated on a small area, this is exactly what happens.

find it quick

Learn more about the physics of a karate chop at **www.findarticles.com/p/articles/mi_m1511**.

The action of breaking a board in a single action is achieved with a great deal of practice. First of all, karate masters have thick calluses on their hands. They toughen their hands by pushing them into containers of sand, rice, or gravel.

Karate masters put their whole strength and concentration into the blow. They hit the board quickly and precisely. The hand is held straight out in a "knife" position, with the side of the hand facing downward, or curled into a fist in a "hammer" position. When seen in slow motion, a board bends before it breaks in two. The upper half of the board squeezes together under the low, while the lower half stretches apart and starts to crack. The crack spreads upward and breaks the board.

When wooden boards are set up for karate demonstrations, they are supported only at the ends. This gives

■ Learners can throw a karate chop at about 20 feet (6 m) per second—just enough to break a 1-inch (2.5-cm) board. A black belt can execute a chop at 46 feet (14 m) per second.

them more room to bend. Breaking boards with bare hands involves both science and experience. Trying it without experience and practice can be dangerous.

Karate Fighting

The study of martial arts, including karate, was born on a small island in Japan called Okinawa. One of the earliest martial arts was a form known as "Te" or "Hand." Today, the form of "Te" is known as "karate," meaning "empty hands."

Science Q&A | Sports

How do animals play a role in sports?

People are not the only athletes. Even before chariots first circled arenas in ancient Rome, humans have used animals in sports.

In ancient Greece, Pakistan, and Africa, the sport of bull vaulting was popular. Cave paintings show that acrobats would catch a running bull by the horns and jump over it from the front to the back. Archaeologists believe either small athletes or children participated in this sport.

Large animals, such as horses and bulls, are still popular in sports. In North America, rodeos draw thousands of people each year. Cowboys test their skills at bronc riding, bareback bronc riding, bull riding, steer wrestling, and calf roping. Horses are used in sports such as show jumping and polo.

In history and throughout the world, people have used animals in races. In ancient Egypt, dogs were used to chase wild animals. In South Africa, there are ostrich races. In Egypt and northeast Africa, camels race against one another.

Homing pigeons can be trained to return to their homes when released from a distant place. When the modern Olympic

■ Sled dogs need to have two major qualities, endurance and speed.

Games started in 1896, homing pigeons were used to carry messages of the event results back to the home countries. Today, pigeon racing is a popular sport.

Dogsled races are held every year in Alaska. Participants race teams of dogs over 1,165 miles (1,875 km) of ice and snow. The dogs often wear boots to protect their paws from ice.

Winter Run

The Iditarod is a famous dogsled race. Competitors travel 1,150 miles (1,850 km) from Anchorage, Alaska, to Nome, Alaska, in winter. The fastest time for completing the race is 9 days, 5 hours.

What are extreme sports?

Many athletes enjoy sports that allow them to be close to the environment. Some athletes even like the challenge of competing with elements in the environment. They find the challenges they are looking for by participating in "extreme" sports.

find it quick

Visit **pbskids.org/kws/sports/equestrian.html** to know more about the sport of show jumping.

■ Sports such as river rafting pit people against the pressure of water flowing in full force.

Extreme sports include rock climbing, snowboarding, skydiving, mountain biking, motorcross, scuba diving, hang gliding, and bungee jumping. Athletes use special equipment to reach heights and speeds that might seem dangerous to most of us. They might also venture into wilderness areas with rough terrain.

Rock climbers face the challenge of scaling mountains and cliffs. Snowboarders and back-country skiers, who ski downhill in unpatrolled areas, race on deep snow where avalanches might occur. Skydivers jump from great heights. Mountain bikers ride on rocky ground, up and down hills, for long distances.

The Eco-Challenge is an extreme sporting event in which teams of athletes race across large wilderness areas using rafts, kayaks, mountain bikes, horses, and their feet. Their only guide is a map and compass. Part of the goal of this race is to promote responsible use of the outdoor environment. All competitors in the Eco-Challenge must follow certain rules. For example, racers can only camp and travel where permitted, and they are not allowed to light campfires.

What are human machines?

Scientists who study how the human body moves think of athletes' bodies as machines.

find it quick

Learn more about biomechanics at
www.topendsports.com/biomechanics.

■ Biomechanics applies the laws of mechanics and physics to human performance.

One area of science looks at sports from a mechanical point of view. This area is called biomechanics. Using high-speed cameras and computer programs, these scientists are able to analyze body movements in detail. They can show problems with techniques and how to fix them for better performance. One test in biomechanics uses a treadmill. Silver dots are attached to an athlete, such as a runner, at points along the body. These dots reflect light onto a high-speed camera. As the athlete runs on the treadmill, the camera takes pictures of the moving dots. The pictures are analyzed by a computer. The computer program shows whether the athlete is running in the best way possible, and gives information about what can be done to improve performance. Even small changes in movement can make a difference in running speed. The test measures length of stride, foot placement, leg speed, and the way in which the athlete lifts his or her knees.

Are kids more prone to injury than adults?

Growing children need to be careful when they play sports and exercise. Teenagers are especially vulnerable to injury.

find it quick

Learn more about prevention of sports injuries at **www.kidshealth.org/parent/firstaid_safe**.

■ Rugby injury rates are reported to be nearly three times higher than soccer and football.

Broken bones, strains, sprains, tendonitis, and shin splints are some of the injuries that happen more frequently in growing children than in adults. They are often caused by overuse of a body part while playing a sport.

Children and teenagers grow very quickly. During growth spurts, their bones can grow faster than the muscles that make them move. This makes joints less flexible, so young people have a greater chance of being injured.

Activities that cause the most injuries to young people between the ages of 5 and 14 are bicycle riding, football, games using playground equipment, baseball, and basketball.

Sports Careers

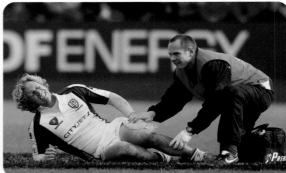

Coaching

If you like sports and enjoy working with people, you may want to become an athletics coach. A coach is a person who helps athletes train, practice, and become better at whatever sport they do. He or she may decide what is the best physical training program for a particular sport. A coach also works with an athlete who is practicing, and helps him or her learn how to move in the best way. For team sports, the coach decides which players will play and gives the team strategies that will help them win the game.

A person who used to be an athlete and knows about a sport can become a coach.

Sports medicine

Sports medicine is a special branch of medicine that helps athletes stay fit. If you are interested in biology, medicine, sports, and working with people, sports medicine may be a career choice for you.

Doctors, physical therapists, and other health care professionals help prevent and treat sports injuries. Athletic trainers help athletes build physical fitness to improve their athletic skills. Trainers also work with athletic teams and provide first aid to injured players. Sports psychologists help athletes develop good mental attitude and overcome stress.

find it quick

Learn more about careers in sports at **http://careerplanning.about.com/ od/occupations/a/sports_industry.htm**.

Young scientists at work

Here is a sports-related science experiment for you to try.

FACT

Salt water is more dense than fresh water because it contains dissolved salt.

TEST

Find two jars, one large, one small. Fill the small jar with 1 cup (250 milliliters) of tap water. Fill the large jar half full with salt water. To make salt water, use 1 cup (250 mL) of warm or hot water from the tap, then mix in 2 tablespoons (30 mL) of salt. Stir until all of the salt is dissolved.

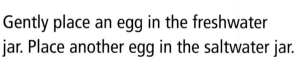

Gently place an egg in the freshwater jar. Place another egg in the saltwater jar.

PREDICT

What has happened to the two eggs? Why?

Now, remove the egg from the freshwater jar. Pour some of the fresh water into the big saltwater jar, adding it gently down the inside of the jar. Keep adding water slowly. What happens?

Answers

The egg in the fresh water should fall to the bottom of the jar. The egg in the salt water should float. By adding more fresh water to the salt water, the egg will gradually be suspended in the middle of the water.

Take a science survey

How healthy are you? Do you think you are as fit as you can be? Young people need regular exercise, good food, and lots of sleep in order to stay healthy and grow strong.

1. How often do you exercise or play sports?

2. What exercise or sports do you do?

3. How long do you play?

4. What kind of food do you eat each day?

5. How much water do you drink?

6. How much sleep do you get each night?

Survey Results

What did you find out? Most growing kids need at least 20 to 30 minutes of moderate exercise each day. Young people need to eat nutritious food everyday. The USDA food guide says people need 5 to 8 grain products each day, 2 to 4 servings of fruit, 3 to 5 servings of vegetables, 2 to 3 milk products, and 2 to 3 meat or meat alternatives. Young people need to eat in the middle range of these numbers of servings. Young people need at least 8 to 10 hours of sleep each night.

Fast Facts

Historians have found a stone carving of a skier in a cave in Norway that is 4,000 years old.

In 1988, Yves Pol of France set a world record for running 3.1 miles (5 km) backward.

The stopwatch was invented in the middle of the 19th century. It made accurate readings of athletic and sport records possible.

The first games of hockey were played by aboriginal North Americans. They played a game called ice shinny on frozen lakes and rivers.

Before football helmets were worn, players let their hair grow long and knotted it across the tops of their heads to form a cushion.

The longest tug-of-war in the world took place in 1889. Two teams in India competed for 2 hours and 41 minutes.

Some South Africans play a unique kind of hockey. It is called octopush, and it is hockey played underwater. They play the game with miniature hockey sticks and a hockey puck on the bottom of a swimming pool.

The first marathon was run by a soldier in 490 BC. Right after the Battle of Marathon against the Persian army, the soldier ran 26 miles (42 km) from Marathon to Athens to tell about the Greeks' victory.

Legend says that golf first began in the hills of Scotland when a bored shepherd began hitting small, round stones into nearby rabbit holes with his staff.

The youngest golfer ever to get a hole in one was only 4 years old.

Glossary

aerobic: requiring the presence of air or free oxygen for life

anaerobic: living in the absence of air or free oxygen

fast-twitch fibers: muscle fibers that contract faster than slow muscles but which fatigue more quickly

fiberglass: a covering material made of glass fibers in resins

homing pigeon: a variety of pigeon bred to be able to find its way home over extremely long distances

hydration: the process of providing an adequate amount of liquid to bodily tissues

hypothalamus: an integral part of the substance of the brain

Olympic Games: a modern international sports competition, held once every four years

slow-twitch fibers: muscle fibers that contract relatively slowly and are resistant to fatigue

Index

aerodynamics 33
athlete 4, 7, 9, 11, 19, 20, 21, 24, 25, 27, 33, 34, 35, 36, 37, 38, 39, 40, 41, 44, 47

biomechanics 40, 41
boomerang 14, 15

electrolytes 23
energy 7, 8, 9, 13, 16, 17, 23

fibers 6, 7, 21

injuries 11, 19, 42, 43, 44

marathon 7, 47
minerals 23
muscles 6, 7, 8, 9, 11, 23, 25, 43

oxygen 7, 8, 9

spandex 21
steroids 24, 25
surfer 28, 29